The Housing Trap

How Buyers Are Captured And Abused
And How To Defend Yourself

Patrick Killelea

http://patrick.net

First Edition, September 2012

Patrick can be contacted at p@patrick.net He is happy to be interviewed and to speak in public about the housing market. Please also email him corrections and suggestions for future editions this book.

Patrick Killelea is not a real estate agent, broker, Realtor® (yuck!), lawyer, or accountant, and has no professional training outside of engineering. This entire book is just his personal opinions. You'd be a fool to take this book as professional advice, so don't, because it isn't. If you need professional legal or real estate advice, see a lawyer. A list of real estate lawyers is provided at:

http://patrick.net/real_estate_lawyers.php

Additional copies of this book can be ordered from Amazon.com. The book is priced at $12.50 so that ordering two copies gets you free Super Saver shipping.

Dedicated to the members of the Patrick.net forum.

We are much smarter together than any one of us is alone.

Special thanks to forum members APOCALYPSEFUCK is Shostakovich, Auntiegrav, B.A.C.A.H., Bap33, Bellingham Bill, bmwman91, bob2356, bubblesitter, corntrollio, Dan8267, E-man, EBGuy, elliemae, errc, FortWayne, freak80, Goran_K, HousingWatcher, iwog, JodyChunder, justme, Kevin, leo707, Malkovich, marcus, uomo_senza_nome, Peter P, pkennedy, PockyClipsNow, Randy H, Robber Baron Elite Scum, robertoaribas, rootvg, Sface, skibum, tatupu70, thomas.wong1986, thunderlips11, Tom Stone, tovarichpeter, tts, Vicente, and ¥ for your many helpful and entertaining comments.

Table of Contents

*But, ah, think what you do when you run in debt;
you give to another power over your liberty. If you
cannot pay at the time, you will be ashamed to see
your creditor; you will be in fear when you speak
to him, you will make poor pitiful sneaking
excuses, and by degrees come to lose your
veracity, and sink into base downright lying; for,
as Poor Richard says, the second vice is lying, the
first is running in debt.*

— Benjamin Franklin in Poor Richard's Almanac

Trapped!

Why do you obey your boss? Why do you suffer
the boring commute to and from work each day?
Why can't you just quit your job, take a few years
off, and enjoy your life?

If you're like most people, the reason is that you
took out a mortgage to buy a house. Once you are
in debt, you are trapped. You are transformed from
a free human being into an obedient servant. If you
don't obey your boss to get money to pay the
mortgage, eventually men with guns will come to
your door and physically remove you and your
family from the house. You won't be able to get
help from the police, because those men removing
you will **be** the police. You're trapped.

A situation where you must obey orders or have to
deal with armed men doing bad things to you and
your family sounds a lot like slavery. If you
complain, you'll be blamed for having taken on the

mortgage. After all, you signed the mortgage papers, didn't you?

How did this happen? Who told you it was a good idea to take on a debt that, even under good conditions, will take 30 years of your working life to pay off?

There is an extensive food chain of people and institutions that drink the blood, sweat, and tears of house buyers, and they all told you it was a good idea to feed them. **You are their food.**

There is no one at all on the buyer's side except the buyer himself and this little book, which is the distillation of years of discussion on the Patrick.net forums. See http://patrick.net to join in the discussion.

Can't Sell

As soon as you buy a house, you have a large loss: you cannot sell and get back the money you just paid.

First, you probably just paid the highest price of anyone interested in the house, so no one else is willing to pay as much as you did.

Second, the commissions involved in selling mean you're instantly 6% in the hole as soon as you buy.

Third, you probably blew a lot of money on the mortgage points and fees, the inspection, the appraisal, etc., putting you even further in the hole.

The net result is that you can't sell unless you come up with a lot of cash to burn. It also means you cannot move to take a better job elsewhere.

Can't Pay Off Mortgage

You can't pay off the mortgage either. If you could pay it all off right now, you wouldn't have borrowed the money to begin with. Now the mortgage is your constant companion.

> *Interest never sleeps nor sickens nor dies; it never goes to the hospital; it works on Sundays and holidays; it never takes a vacation; it never visits nor travels; it takes no pleasure; it is never laid off work nor discharged from employment; it never works on reduced hours. Once in debt, interest is your companion every minute of the day and night; you cannot shun it or slip away from it; you cannot dismiss it; it yields neither to entreaties, demands, or orders; and whenever you get in its way or cross its course or fail to meet its demands, it crushes you.*
> *– J. Reuben Clark*

Must Keep Obeying Boss

Your only course of action is to keep obeying your

boss because you need the money to pay the mortgage. You're trapped, and that was their plan all along.

> *The Mexican Dream is to escape from debt peonage. The American Dream is to get **into** debt peonage.*

None of this applies if you're very rich or very poor. If you're very rich, you can just pay cash and not care if the house price goes down. If you're very poor, go ahead and max out your mortgage debt. You can't pay it back anyway. You'll probably get a few years of living in a nice house that you can't afford before the bank finally throws you out, and you have no other assets to confiscate, so no harm done.

This book is for the people in the middle, which is most of us.

The Conspirators

Who told you to get into debt to buy a house? Everyone who stood to make money off you! They all told you to get into debt, and a few more people besides, including some people very close to you, and some people very high up. Let's go over the conspirators who helped to trap you.

Your Agent

As a buyer, your own real estate agent is your worst enemy. His financial motive is to get you to take out the maximum mortgage and to spend as much as possible as quickly as possible. Why? Because he gets paid nothing if you do not buy, and he gets paid more if you overpay for a house.

Those two perverse incentives neatly combine to give your agent a powerful motive to push you into grossly overbidding, because that gives him a greater chance that your offer will be accepted, so that he can quickly gain the maximum profit from your mistake.

Your agent's financial motives are the *exact opposite* of your best interest.

Agents take 100 billion dollars each year in commissions from buyers. Agents point out that the seller writes their commission check, but they always fail to mention that the seller gets that money from the buyer. Who brings the money to the table - the seller or the buyer? The buyer. All money comes from buyers. No buyer, no money.

Even if we politely agree that the seller writes the commission check, doesn't that payment then show who your agent is really working for?

Your agent has the means, motive, and opportunity to cheat you. For example, you have no way of knowing whether your agent is lying about the other offers he tells you to bid against. Those offers can very easily be faked to push you to bid higher. You never get to see or confirm any of the other bids under the current system, if there even are any other real bids. There should be a law to make all bids public and validated by a bank, but the NAR passes out generous "campaign donations" to so many Congressmen and state legislators that you should not expect any changes soon.

One Patrick.net forum reader:

> When I'm told that the seller has multiple offers, I tell the broker that we've also put offers on several other houses. Fear of loss works both ways.

Another:

> 16 other offers? How can I know for sure that there is really even one other

13

offer? So you're telling me that I should base the biggest financial decision of my life on the honesty and integrity of Realtors®?

A third:

Never trust a single word from a realtor. They are constantly lying that "I heard there's another offer, make your highest offer" or "The bank has a verbal with someone, but if you come in with a strong offer they might take it." They don't seem to understand that I want a deal, there's no reason to get in a bidding war over any particular property in this market, and if one owner isn't willing to consider a low bid, there's a house right down the street for sale too. As soon as I told one agent I didn't want to make an offer if there was a second bidder, that bidder mysteriously disappeared and he claimed he mis-heard the information and there wasn't anyone else.

In 2012, a Realtor® published a humorous and honest but negative review of a house on the Patrick.net "Open House Reviews" forum. When the seller saw this review of his property and complained, the Realtor® was promptly fired by his agency. Why was he fired? For giving his honest opinion! Another Realtor® on the forum defended the firing, saying that giving your honest opinion of a property in public violates the Realtor® code of "ethics," unless you are saying only positive things about the house. What kind of ethics are those?

When any agent praises a house as a good deal, you should be very wary. If a house were really a good deal, your agent or a friend of his would have already bought it. Why should he let **you** get a good deal which he could get for himself? Agents know about every house before it's publicly listed, which is long before you know about it. The MLS (Multiple Listing Service, a private network of databases controlled by real estate agents) system gives agents first crack at every house, so you get to look only at the overpriced leftovers that your agent and his friends do not want, so you would be wise to assume that **every MLS-listed house is a bad deal**.

Your best chance of finding a good deal is by looking at the listings the agents do not want to show you: FSBO (For Sale By Owner) sites, probate court, foreclosures, and builder inventory.

Your agent's reluctance to deal with any of these is proof that he is not on your side. If your agent cannot make a commission, you will not be shown the house.

Every commission-based agent reads from the same script. Their job is to manipulate you to into accepting one of the invariably bad deals listed on the MLS so that they can get a commission out of you quickly. Their job is **not** to get you a good deal.

There are agents who really believe they are helping the buyer, but they're in denial about their conflict of interest. Author Upton Sinclair had a great explanation for that:

> *It is difficult to get a man to understand something when his salary depends on not understanding it.*

Imagine you're looking for a hotel room while traveling, and someone comes up to you saying they will happily help you find a hotel room, and that their services are free. That person is a **tout**, someone who is paid to solicit your business but pretends to be helping you. Do you think a tout is really looking out for your best interest and is going to get you the best deal on a hotel room? No way. He will take you to the hotel that gives him the biggest kickback. Commission-based buyer's agents are nothing more than touts. Avoid them.

Why should you give up nearly a year of your life to pay salesmen who are working against your best interests? Together, the buyer's agent and the seller's agent take a 6% commission. That 6% commission means 6% of the 30 years of your working life it takes to pay off a house. Say half your time at work is just to pay the mortgage. That's 0.06 x 30 x 0.5 = 0.9 years, almost a whole year of donating your labor to real estate agents. Just find a house on your own, hopefully a house for sale by owner, and get a real estate lawyer who is paid by the hour to draw up the offer and complete the sale. Hiring a lawyer is much safer than using an agent, and likely to be much cheaper too. See http://patrick.net/real_estate_lawyers.php for a list of real estate lawyers in your area.

Agents are experts at manipulating buyers to get them to put their foot in the trap, since that's the agent's only real job. Buyers on the other hand tend to be young and inexperienced. There is a huge asymmetry of information.

Seller's agents are no better than buyer's agents at promoting the interests of their clients. A famous study by economist Stephen Dubner showed that agents get higher prices when selling their own houses than when selling clients' houses, and a 2008 study by Consumers Reports showed that on average, sellers without an agent get their asking price, but **sellers who use an agent get $5,000 less than asking price for their house** and then have to pay the 6% commission on top of that! Selling a house with an agent is like paying someone to rob you.

Everybody hates house-agents because they have everybody at a disadvantage. All other callings have a certain amount of give and take; the house agent simply takes. – H G Wells

Your Mortgage Broker

Your mortgage broker is also conspiring against you. Mortgage brokers take a percentage of the loan, so they want you to take out the biggest loan possible to maximize their commission. And just like real estate brokers, mortgage brokers get paid according to how bad the deal is for you. The worse the deal is for you the borrower (higher interest rate, points, fees, etc) the more the mortgage broker gets!

For proof, look up Yield Spread Premium, or YSP, which is the bonus paid to your mortgage broker in exchange for getting you to agree to a higher interest rate than you actually qualify for.

Your Bank

Your bank also wants you to get into as much debt as possible without defaulting. If you pay a low price for a house and manage to avoid all debt, then the banks lose the interest you would have paid and their control over you. Debt-free citizens are not profitable to banks. Your debt is their wealth.

Banks are the arms merchants in an eternal war of debt between buyers. Whichever buyer takes on more debt and moves closer to the edge of bankruptcy gets to live in the house, at least until he can't make the payments anymore. This arms race of debt puts responsible savers at a disadvantage, but it benefits the banks with fees and interest. The banks' sole fear is not getting bailed out when loans that it couldn't sell to Fannie or Freddie go bad. Fortunately for the biggest banks, they are guaranteed bailouts at public expense via the Federal Reserve.

Fannie And Freddie

Government agencies like Fannie Mae, Freddie Mac, and the FHA love your mortgage debt, because their own existence (and more importantly, their executive salaries) depends on guaranteeing private loans with public money.

Fannie and Freddie are perhaps the largest scam ever devised. Most people will unwisely borrow as much as possible to buy a house. The existence of Fannie and Freddie just allows buyers to borrow more money than the free market would offer by pushing the default risk onto taxpayers. This benefits bankers with lower risk, but harms buyers with higher house prices and harms taxpayers with repayment obligations when buyers default. Ironically, Fannie and Freddie drive up debt, the cost of housing, and taxes in the name of "affordability." The public is unlikely to ever understand this. It is the perfect crime.

The banks sold millions of bad loans to Fannie Mae and Freddie Mac during the bubble, putting taxpayers on the hook for the banks' gambling losses. Yet banks get to keep all the profits on their good loans. Heads they win, tails **you** lose.

The Federal Reserve

The Federal Reserve, also known as "The Fed," is a private banking cartel created in a secret meeting on Jekyll Island in 1913 to guarantee that their members will be bailed out with newly printed money whenever they get into trouble. The Federal Reserve is not federal, and it has no reserves. It is private and just has a printing press and the general ignorance of the public about why it really exists. The Fed has printed so much money that the US dollar is now worth less than 5% of what it was worth in 1913. These days, the Fed doesn't even have to physically print. It just credits new money directly onto banks' balance sheets via a few keystrokes at a computer terminal.

The Federal Reserve creates this money to protect the biggest banks from responsibility for their own bad decisions, at the expense of the public, all in the name of "financial stability." So we see the Fed printing cash to buy up bad mortgages – which weakens everyone's wealth by inflating the currency – to get the banks off the hook. This slows down buyer-friendly deflation in housing prices.

Banks get to keep any profits they make, but bank losses just get passed on to you and me as extra cost added onto the price of a house when the Fed prints up money and buys their bad mortgages. If the Fed did not prevent the free market from working, you would be able to buy a house much more cheaply. Bank profits are privatized and bank losses are socialized. Good work if you can get it. The Federal Reserve is nothing short of a criminal conspiracy to protect the banker class at the expense of the rest of us.

Newspapers

Newspapers earn money from advertising placed by real estate agents, lenders, and mortgage brokers. Papers are pressured by that money to publish the real estate industry's self-serving housing forecasts. Worse, real estate agents have a near-monopoly on actual housing offer and sale price "facts," and newspaper reporters **never** ask agents hard questions like "How do we know you're not lying about those sales?"

It turns out they were indeed lying about those sales. Blogger Michael Olenick's personal investigations resulted in the NAR's being forced to restate sales data significantly downward for the years 2007 to 2011. It is a good thing that Mr. Olenick investigated where mainstream reporters would not, because the entire US government accepts and uses NAR data without ever questioning it.

> *NAR data is the sole benchmark for existing home sales in the monthly scorecard released by the Dept. of Housing and Urban Development (HUD), under supervision of the White House. As of Nov., 2011, the NAR statistics are the exclusive measure used to measure existing home sales, a vital component used by government agencies, banks, economists, and others to gauge the health of the housing market. Additionally, the data has been cited by the Dept. of the Treasury and various branches of the Federal Reserve. – Michael Olenick*

The pro-agent bias in the mainstream media results in an endless stream of stories reporting that real estate agents say it's a good time to buy. Real estate agents are nothing more than used-house salesmen. Reporting that used-house salesmen say it's a good time to buy a house is like reporting that used-car salesmen says it's a good time to buy a used car. It's not news, it's advertising.

Newspapers almost always refer to rising house prices as a "better" housing market, and falling house prices as a "worse" housing market.

> *Saying it is "good" for housing prices to rise is saying that it is good for*

housing to take an increasing share of salaries each year, forever. There's a limit, and it is somewhat shy of 100%.
– Patrick.net reader Bryce N.

The NAR

The National Association of Realtors® (NAR) is supposedly a "trade association" but a better description is that it is a lobbying group dedicated to keeping buyers and sellers trapped in the commission system to preserve Realtor® profits. The majority of real estate agents are members of the NAR, but not all of them are.

The NAR has nearly one million members, making the biggest trade association in the country, with awful power to twist state laws regarding real estate. According to the Federal Trade Commission, "State officials have offered the opinion that virtually no proposed legislation relating to real estate has a chance of passage unless it is approved by the state association of Realtors."

Most regulation of real estate is done via state law and state real estate commissions, theoretically aimed at protecting the public. But in reality, nearly all state laws and regulatory bodies covering real estate exist to **prevent alternative business models from threatening agent commissions**. According to the Consumer Federation of America, more than 70% of real estate commissioners are real estate brokers or salesmen, an immense and ongoing conflict of interest which is **never** mentioned in the mainstream press.

The NAR is only part of the lobbying problem though. There are other powerful financial interests which corrupt our laws to help trap you, such as The National Association of Home Builders and the National Association of Mortgage Brokers.

Congress

Many if not all members of Congress and state legislatures get bribes (also called *campaign donations*) from the NAR and from the banks. When the NAR and banks give out large amounts of money, they obviously expect something valuable in return. What they expect and get is that laws will be aimed squarely at increasing commissions to Realtors® and increasing interest payments to banks. Buyers like you lose, because you have no lobbyists in DC.

According to Opensecrets.org, the NAR is the 4th largest overall donor to congressional campaigns.

As if that were not enough corruption, Congress authorized vast amounts of TARP bailout cash taken from taxpayers to be loaned directly to the worst-run banks, banks that already gambled on bad mortgages and lost. The Fed and Congress are letting the banks "extend and pretend" that their mortgage loans will get paid back.

The government pretends to be interested in affordable housing, but when housing is becoming truly affordable via falling prices, they try to stop it, using taxpayer money to prop up prices. Their actions speak louder than their words.

The President of The United States

Every president talks about the need to "support" housing prices, meaning the use of government intervention to make you pay more for a house than the free market would. No president ever talks about the harm that artificially high house prices do to young families. You will never hear a president admit that we need **lower house prices**. They talk about "affordability" but what they mean is increased mortgage debt. Increased debt is not affordability. Americans should be encouraged to save, not to get into debt.

Every president so far has preferred to sacrifice the young and the poor to benefit the old and the rich, and to make sure bankers have plenty of debt to earn interest on.

Current Owners

Anyone who owns is likely to encourage you to buy too, to prop up his own house value via comps, and so that he can feel that he is not alone in his sinking boat. His fervor is akin to that of the religious zealot who simply cannot stand that you don't believe too, because your disbelief creates doubt in his own mind. Current owners refuse to believe they are wasting huge amounts of money, which means they are wasting many years of their working lives.

The propagation of the owner mentality is very much like the propagation of vampires, which create new vampires by sucking all the blood out of their victims. Once you are an owner, your brain becomes infected by the idea that your own wealth depends on keeping the game going at any cost, so you help to lure yet more young and innocent buyers into the housing trap.

Your Boss

Your boss would like to keep you dependent on the paycheck that he controls so that he can keep controlling you. One of the best ways to keep you dependent is to get you deeply in debt. Your boss wants you to be financially stretched almost to the breaking point, but not past it, since then you might just walk away from your job, which means no control over you at all.

A boss who encourages you to buy an expensive house is not looking out for your best interest. The debt game is a filthy battle for control over your labor. Money is just an abstraction for labor.

You've been trained to take orders and obey people in authority from your first day of kindergarten. School is only partly about learning. The secondary and unspoken goal of schooling is to teach conformity and obedience, which prepares you to take on a mortgage and to obey your boss.

Your Parents

Your parents don't make any money from conspiring against you, but they will tell you to buy because they don't understand that house prices can also fall. In their experience, house prices only went up.

Your Wife's Parents

I almost goes without saying a man is judged by his in-laws based on the size and quality of the house that he buys for their daughter. Evidence of a well-stocked bank account can do wonders to reassure them though.

Your Wife

In almost all human cultures, houses are bought by men for their wives as part of the marriage deal. Your wife usually wants you to buy a nice house to increase her own sense of security and her status among peers. She may even grant or withhold sexual favors to encourage you to move in the direction she wants. Taking on a mortgage for such favors would be the most expensive sex of your life.

Unmarried men who own a house can confirm to you what a turn-on having a house is for women that they date. The counterargument is that showing off large amounts of cash in the bank works equally well, but without the burden of taking on debt. Former HP executive Mark Hurd got into trouble for sexual harassment in 2011 when he tried to pick up an employee by showing her his million-dollar-plus checking account balance on an ATM receipt. His mistake was using this tactic on an employee. Otherwise, his reasoning was sound. Women like financial security in men.

So owning a house or having a big bank balance are both ways to impress women, but having a big bank balance gives you much more flexibility and independence. You're also much more likely to stay happily married in the long run if you never get near the financial abyss of mortgage debt. Financial trouble is the number two cause of divorce. Spousal abuse is the number one cause, and a rise in spousal abuse itself has been linked to the rise in foreclosures.

Rather than possibly divorcing you if you don't buy a house, your wife will almost certainly divorce you if you **do** buy a house and go bankrupt trying to pay the mortgage. She probably won't divorce you for renting a very nice place, and then taking her to Paris for a nice vacation each spring, which you can do just by avoiding that suicidal mortgage.

If your wife is religious, you could also point out Proverbs 22:7:

> *The rich rule over the poor, and the borrower is servant to the lender.*

Or Deuteronomy 28:43-44:

> *[They] will rise above you higher and higher, but you will sink lower and lower. They will make loans to you, but you will not make loans to them. They will be the head, but you will be the tail.*

Real estate agents are experts at manipulating women's emotions to get them to pressure their husbands to buy. For perhaps the most vile example of manipulation of a hapless husband ever set to film, search YouTube for "Suzanne Researched This."

> *Cashtration (n.): The act of buying a house, which renders the subject financially impotent for an indefinite period of time.*

29

Fallacies and Fantasies

Here are the lies, spin, and emotional manipulation which the host of conspirators will use against you, along with replies you can use to defend yourself. Forewarned is forearmed.

Appreciation

"Houses always increase in value, so any commission you pay will be made up in increased value. Appreciation will also cover the monthly loss in cash flow relative to renting."

FALSE. Houses obviously do not always increase in price. Witness the epic housing bubble and crash in the US, and the similar bubble and crash in Japan 15 years earlier. Vast numbers of families were financially devastated because they listened to Realtor® spokesmen telling them to buy. Look up "Lawrence Yun Watch" and "David Lereah Watch" for examples of how those NAR spokesmen led the public to slaughter in the housing market.

Prices fluctuated wildly during the bubble, but values did not. The **value** of a house is constant. It just sits there. You get shelter, but you have to pay property tax and maintenance and the loss of alternative uses of capital for every moment you own the house. A house is a dead asset. The **price** of a house rises with salary inflation, but house prices cannot increase more than salaries in the long run. This is obvious if you think about it.

For example, prices in the Netherlands are about the same as they were 350 years ago, in terms of how many years of work it takes to buy a house. Warren Buffett and Charles Schwab have both pointed out that houses do not increase in intrinsic value. Unless there's a bubble or a crash, house prices simply reflect current salaries, interest rates, and lending standards.

Consider a 100 year old house. Its value in sheltering you is exactly the same as it was 100 years ago. It did not increase in value at all. It did not spontaneously get bigger, or renovate itself. Quite the opposite - the house drained cash from its owners for 100 years of maintenance, taxes, and insurance - costs that never go away. The price of the house went up about as much as salaries went up, which is about the same as the quantity of dollars printed by the Federal Reserve went up.

My grandmother used to complain about the cost of milk. "Why, when I was a girl, a gallon of milk cost a dime! Just look at how much people are overcharging for milk now." I asked her how much people got paid back then. "Oh, about $15 a week", came the reply. This sounds very much like the reasoning people use now when they talk about how much their father's house appreciated "in the long run" without considering that inflation rose just as much because the Federal Reserve debased the US dollar.

As long as unemployment remains high, salary inflation is unlikely, and salary inflation the only kind of inflation that boosts house prices. Inflation in everything else (food, energy, medical) just takes away from the money people have to spend on housing.

Real estate agents, after years of blathering about how house prices only go up, are finally faced with the incontrovertible reality that house prices also go down.

Building Equity

"Renters have no opportunity to build equity."

FALSE. If someone tells you that you are not building equity by renting, reply that you are not **losing** equity either. Then you should point out that you are in fact building equity from the return on your investments. Even if you're not making much, it is still better to get a low interest rate on cash than to own a depreciating asset.

Equity is just money. Renters are actually in a far better position to build equity than owners are, just by saving the money that owners are wasting on mortgages, taxes, maintenance, insurance, and the loss of investment income. Renters are getting paid to wait, both in the monthly savings from renting rather than owning and in the pleasure of watching the value of their investments increase.

How do owners lose more than renters? Let us count the ways.

Owners lose every month when they pay more in ownership expenses than they would pay in rent. The mortgage interest deduction does not save anyone any money, but rather just causes prices to be higher than they otherwise would be.

Owners lose principal in a leveraged way when prices decline. A 4% price decline completely wipes out all the equity of "owners" who actually own only 10% of their house. Remember that the agents will take 6% if they possibly can.

Owners must pay property taxes simply to own a house. That is not true of stocks, bonds, or any other asset that can build equity. Only houses are such a guaranteed drain on cash.

Owners must insure a house, but not financial investments like stocks or bonds.

Owners must pay to repair a house, but not a stock or a bond.

The simple fact is that the renter - if willing to save and invest his money - can buy a house for cash in

less than half the time that a conventional buyer can pay off a mortgage. Interest generally accounts for about half of the cost of a house. The renter who saves not only pays no interest, but also gets interest on his savings, even if just a little. Leveraged housing appreciation, often presented as the "secret" to wealth, cannot be counted on, and can just as easily work against the buyer. In fact, that leverage is the danger that got current buyers into trouble.

As we saw, if a buyer puts 10% down and the house goes down 4%, he has lost 100% of his money on paper. If he has to sell due to job loss or a mortgage rate adjustment, he lost 100% in the real world.

> *Why do the buy side idiots ALWAYS fall for the FALSE CHOICE FALLACY????*
> *Choice 1: Buy today, right now, this second.*
> *Choice 2: Rent until you die.*
> *Um, I'll take door #3: let prices fall another couple hundred $K on a home like this, and buy it in a year or two.*
> *–Patrick.net reader Roberto Aribas*

Renters Throw Money Away

"Renting is just throwing your money away."

FALSE. Owners can easily throw away much

more money than renters, for the same sort of house in the same location, especially in nicer neighborhoods.

If you don't own a house but want to live in one, your choice is to rent a house or **rent money** to buy a house. To rent money is to take out a loan. A mortgage is a money-rental agreement. House renters take no financial risk at all, but money-renting owners take on the huge risk of falling house prices, as well as obligating themselves to pay all the costs of repairs, insurance, property taxes, etc.

Even if you buy outright for cash, you're still renting the house to yourself, losing alternative uses of that money, and taking the risk of falling house prices. You have to compare the details of owning to renting to know the right thing to do. Try the rent vs buy calculator at http://patrick.net/calculator.php You can use it to figure out the approximate right price to pay for a house based on what it would cost to rent, your income tax rate, and other factors. You'll see that renting is frequently much cheaper than owning the same quality house, especially in expensive neighborhoods.

To summarize: if you don't rent, you either:

1. Have a mortgage, in which case you are throwing away money on interest, tax, insurance, maintenance, and the loss of investment income on

your equity.

Or

2. Own outright, in which case you are throwing away the investment income you could have gotten on your equity by converting your house to cash, investing in bonds, and renting a similar place to live for less money. This extra income could be enough to retire on right now.

Either way, owners usually lose more money every month than renters. Currently, yearly rents in the San Francisco Bay Area are about 3% of the cost of buying an equivalent house. This means a house is returning about 3% rent minus taxes, maintenance, and insurance, bringing the landlord's return down to 0%.

Those landlords are loaning a house to their tenants at a 3% interest rate, called rent. This is a fantastic deal for renters. When it is possible to borrow a million dollar house for 3% yearly rent at the same time a loan of a million dollars in cash costs 5% interest, plus 1.3% property tax, plus 1% maintenance, something is clearly broken. Renters are enjoying an extreme discount at the landlord's expense.

If someone tells you that you are throwing money away by renting, you can reply "The landlord is giving me a huge gift. He's subsidizing me to live in his rental. I'll take free money any day."

The above analysis does not even consider the obvious risk that the property will decline in price. Renters are completely protected from the current massive equity losses that owners are experiencing. Here's a great quote from an NPR interview with an underwater owner:

> *We would do it [pay the mortgage] if the equity was there, but in a case where we're already so behind... Imagine that for five years, say, we're gonna pay four grand a month and then we're just gonna be back up at what we bought the house for. We feel like **we're throwing away money**.*

Tax Deduction

"There are tax advantages to owning."

FALSE. There is a theoretical tax benefit for high-income couples with expensive houses and big mortgages, but unfortunately for them, the higher price of the house completely wipes out that benefit in reality. The price simply gets bid up by all the other high-income bidders who are also counting on that deduction. Only the banks really benefit from the deduction, by increasing the amount of mortgage debt they can earn interest on.

There is not even any theoretical tax benefit to owning for modest-income couples in modest houses. Every married couple filing jointly automatically gets to subtract the standard $11,900 deduction from their adjusted gross income to arrive at their taxable income. Alternately, you may add up modest deductions in seven categories: Medical, Taxes, Interest, Charity, Casualty and Theft, Job Expenses, and Other Misc. If the total of your expenses in these categories exceeds the standard deduction, you can itemize them on Schedule A of your tax return to reduce your taxable income.

Let's assume that your only deductible expenses fall into the Taxes and Interest categories. Taxes mainly include the income tax you pay to the state (or its sales tax) and the property taxes on your house or other non-investment real estate. In a high-tax state like New Jersey, you might easily pay $7,200 in property taxes and $700 in income taxes, for a total of $7,900. So the first $4,000 of interest expenses just brings your deductions up to the standard $11,900, without reducing your taxable income at all. It's only the interest above $4,000 that you can deduct.

For a high-income couple, let's assume they can itemize their state income tax of $3,400, charitable contributions of $1,000, and medical expenses of $1,000. These deductions use up $5,400 of the $11,900 standard deduction. So the first $6,500 of property taxes and interest saves them nothing. After that, their savings depend on their tax bracket, which could be as high as 35 percent for a certain segment of income, but is limited by the Alternative Minimum Tax (AMT) and the limit on total mortgage debt.

Interest is paid in real dollars that buyers suffered to earn. That money is really entirely gone, even if the buyer didn't pay income tax on those dollars before spending them on mortgage interest. You don't get rich spending a dollar to save 35 cents!

Buyers do not ever "get interest back" at tax time. If a buyer gets an income tax refund, that's just because he overpaid his taxes, giving the government an interest-free loan. The rest of us are grateful.

Real Estate Is Local

"All real estate is local, so you cannot say anything about the national market. This particular neighborhood will always do fine."

FALSE. Lending is global. When interest rates go up, mortgages are harder to get everywhere. This will push prices down everywhere.

Agents used to love to say that house prices had never decreased nationally in America. They don't say that anymore.

So Little Supply

"There's so little supply available right now. You

must raise your bid to be competitive."

FALSE. Agents love to claim there is very little supply no matter what the state of the market is. In reality, every single house is always potentially for sale. Every house has a price, all the time, even if it's not being advertised. Pay that price, and the house is yours.

But let's say that the list of houses your agent is showing you as being on the market right now is small. How do you know that list is complete? Perhaps your agent has strategically omitted the houses being sold through other agencies, and all the foreclosures, probate sales, FSBOs, and new construction.

Your agent may also claim that increases in real estate supply are slow, since it can take a builder more than a year to build a house. Just point out that every for-sale sign in a yard **instantly** increases the supply of houses on the market. There is no need to wait for builders.

So Many Buyers

"As soon as prices drop a little, the number of buyers on the sidelines willing to jump back in increases."

FALSE. There are very few buyers out there relative to the total housing stock, and they are limited by the increasing difficulty of borrowing as the government gets wary of ever-increasing bank bailouts.

No one ever has to buy, but there will be more and more people who have no choice but to sell as their payments rise when their adjustable loans reset. That will keep driving prices downward for a long time.

Foreigners

"Rich foreigners are driving up housing prices."

FALSE. Most American housing is clearly a bad investment at this point. Foreigners can just wait and watch American housing continue to fall, and then buy for much less in a few years. Rich foreign investors are not dumb enough to pay the "idiot tax" of buying into a badly overpriced market, but your agent is hoping that you are.

House Prices Don't Fall To Zero

"House prices don't fall to zero like stock prices, so it's safer to invest in real estate."

FALSE. It's true that house prices generally do not fall to zero, but **your** equity in a house can easily fall to zero and then way past zero deep into the red. Even a fall of only 4% completely wipes out everyone who has only 10% equity in their house because agents will take 6% if they can trap that seller with a contract. This means that house price crashes are actually worse than stock crashes. Most people unwisely have most of their money in their house, and that money is dangerously leveraged.

Supply And Demand

"Housing prices are driven by supply and demand."

FALSE. Housing prices are driven by interest rates, lending standards, and government interference in the free market. The "supply and demand" law says that people buy less as prices rise. This was exactly **wrong** during the bubble! People were willing to pay more for houses because the prices were rising, and banks were willing to lend more because higher prices gave them the illusion of more collateral.

Supply went way up as the builders were fooled about the value of houses just like the banks were, while the average family income fell 2.3% from 2001 to 2004. So prices violated the most basic assumptions about supply and demand.

The Census.gov website has data for Santa Clara County, California for the bubble years of 2000-2003 which shows that the ratio of housing units available per person increased while prices were also rising:

Year	Units	People	Ratio
2000	580,868	1,686,474	0.34
2001	587,013	1,692,299	0.35
2002	592,494	1,677,426	0.35
2003	596,526	1,678,421	0.36

This directly violates the "law" of supply and demand in Santa Clara County. There was an **oversupply** compared to a few years before, yet prices rose!

At a national level, there was a similar story in the bubble years of 2000 to 2005:

Year	Units	People	Ratio
2000	115.9M	281M	0.41
2005	124.6M	295M	0.42

Again there was more housing per person in 2005 than in 2000. So national prices should have fallen, and yet they surged!

The truth is that prices can rise or fall without any change in supply or demand. The bubble was a mania of cheap and easy credit. Now the mania is over. There is huge supply because of overbuilding, and there is less demand now that the baby boomers are retiring and selling. Prices in the housing market are mostly a function of how much the banks are willing to lend, since most people will borrow as much possible, amounts that are completely disconnected from their salaries and disconnected from the rental value of the property. Banks have been willing to accommodate crazy borrowers because banker control of the US government means that banks can push losses onto taxpayers through government housing agencies like the FHA, or onto every holder of US dollars via the Federal Reserve.

Land Shortage

"They aren't making any more land."

TRUE, but America has plenty of land, far more than we need for our population. Anyway, it is always possible to overpay for a house, no matter how little land there may be.

Japan actually does have a severe land shortage, with close to half the population of the US crammed into a space the size of California, but that hasn't stopped prices from falling in Japan for 22 years straight. Prices in Japan are now back down to the same level they were 25 years ago, because buyers overpaid by so much back then.

Fundamentals Don't Matter

"The Patrick.net calculator says the house I'm

interested in is worth far less than the asking price. That's not very helpful in coming up with an offer."

FALSE. It's very helpful to be able to document that you could be paying much less to live in the same location and same quality house just by renting. It's a great negotiating point.

You can't lose by winning. Renting the same quality house in the same area for much less money every month than the owner pays is winning. Maybe others will get the warm fuzzy feeling of ownership, but you will get the cold hard cash that they are losing.

Commissions Don't Matter

"I'll just amortize the commissions and other transaction costs over 30 years and they'll be OK."

FALSE. The median length of house ownership in America is **six** years, not thirty. That means that half of owners end up selling within six years, so the 7% or so that you'll pay in commission and closing fees comes out to more than 1% of the purchase price per year, and that's a lot of money.

You may think you're different and that you will actually stay put for 30 years, but statistically you're not, and you won't.

Agents Don't Care What You Pay

"The difference between $200,000 and $210,000 is about $300 in commission to the buyer's agent (3% of the $10,000). He doesn't really care about that extra $300."

FALSE. Your agent may not care directly about the extra $300, but he cares **a lot** about whether your offer gets accepted, so that he can get paid as quickly as possible and move on to his next victim. If your agent gets you to bid more than necessary so that your bid definitely comes out on top, then the extra $300 is a bonus that you paid your agent to betray you. The $10,000 you lost by overbidding didn't cost your agent anything.

My Neighborhood Is Different

"Local incomes justify the high prices. Anyway, prices were always way beyond equivalent rent in San Francisco (or whatever expensive town). Higher-income people can afford to spend a larger portion of their income on a mortgage, so your rules of thumb do not apply to them."

FALSE. Most bankers use a multiple of 3 as the maximum safe price-to-income ratio. The price-to-income ratio is still more than 7 in expensive areas like San Francisco and New York City. That's well beyond the danger zone, into the twilight zone.

The price-to-rent ratio in San Francisco and other expensive towns was normal just like anywhere else in 2000. It more than doubled by 2005. (See page 34 of John Talbott's excellent book "Sell Now!")

Even if you can afford to spend more than 7 times your income on a house, that does not mean you should. The cost of renting is usually less than the cost of owning in affluent neighborhoods, making most houses a bad deal for the buyer in these places. The renter living in the same quality house next door pays far less per month.

Wealthy neighborhoods are often deceptive. The majority of mortgages in expensive areas are ARMs (Adjustible Rate Mortgages), and ARMs are not taken out by the rich. People near the border of bankruptcy take out ARMs because they can't afford fixed rate loans. The rich don't have loans at all.

Many of these ARM loans have exceptionally deadly repayment terms, and so are known as "neutron mortgages." Like the neutron bomb, they destroy people, but leave buildings standing. They are also known as "suicide loans."

You Have To Live Somewhere

"You have to live somewhere."

TRUE, but that doesn't mean you should waste

your life savings on a bad investment. You are likely to be able to live in a better house for less money by renting. A renter could save hundreds of thousands of dollars, not only by paying less every month, but also by avoiding the devastating loss of his downpayment.

Rentals Not Available

"It is hard to find a rental that is the equivalent of this house."

PARTIALLY TRUE. Sometimes there just is no equivalent rental available in the same area. Placing an ad or talking to neighbors saying you're looking for a rental in that area is often enough to bring new rentals out of the woodwork though.

Rentals All Suck

"If you don't own, you'll live in a dump in a bad neighborhood."

FALSE. In upscale neighborhoods, for any given monthly payment, you can probably rent a nicer house than you can buy. Renters in those areas live better, not worse.

There are downsides to renting, such as being told to move at the end of your lease, or having your rent raised, but millions of people are quite happy renting. There are worse downsides for owners anyway, such as being fired and losing your house, or having your interest rate and property taxes adjust upward. Remember, property taxes and maintenance are forever.

Some people want the mobility that renting affords. Renters can usually get out of a lease and move anywhere they want within a month or two, with no real estate commission. Some of the savviest people in the world are renters. For example, the majority of people in New York City and Switzerland are renters.

Most landlords are happy to let you redecorate the rental to your taste, as long as you are improving the property. The median ownership length for a house is only six years anyway, which is the same as the median rental tenancy length.

Parents of young children should note that is generally cheaper to rent a house in a good school district than to buy a house in the same district.

Plus, the biggest upside of renting is hardly ever mentioned: renters can choose a short commute by living very close to work or to the train line. An extra two hours every day of free time not wasted commuting is the best work bonus you can ever get.

Owners Can Remodel

"Owners can change their houses to suit their tastes."

FALSE. Even single family detached housing is often restricted by Covenants, Conditions, and Restrictions (CCRs) and House Owner's Associations (HOAs). Imagine having to get the approval of some picky neighbor on the Architectural Review Board every time you want to change the color of your trim. Yet that's how most houses are sold these days.

In California, your HOA can and will foreclose on your house without a judicial hearing. They can fine you $100/day for leaving your garage door open, and then foreclose and take your house away if you refuse to pay. In about half of all states, when you join an HOA you also give the HOA the right to foreclose on you.

But The Newspapers Say...

"The newspaper articles and statistics show that prices are not falling in my neighborhood."

FALSE. The house prices in the papers are not complete and have murky origins. Those prices are "estimated" from the county transfer tax and making that tax public record is optional. A buyer who does not want you to see how little he paid has only to ask to put the transfer tax on the back of the deed and it will not show up on computer searches of the deed, which show only the front. Others voluntarily pay more tax than they have to, in order to inflate the apparent price to fool the next buyer. At a tax rate of about $1 per thousand of sale price, as in San Mateo County, California, you have to pay only $100 extra tax to make your purchase price look $100,000 higher.

Even though you can in theory go to your county building and get sale price information, in reality most counties will give it to you in a painfully slow and inconvenient way. For example, in Redwood City, California's county building there are PC's where you can look at data for any particular house, but you cannot print, you cannot save data, and you cannot email data out. All you can do is write prices down manually, one at a time. And that's how real estate interests like it. Your elected representatives are serving them, not you.

As for the obviously biased sources like real estate agents and the NAR, you should assume that their sales price numbers do not include the effective price reductions from "incentives" like upgrades, vacations, cars, assumed mortgages and backroom cash rebates to buyers.

But The Appraiser Said...

"My appraisal proves that my house is worth what I paid for it."

FALSE. Appraisers simply compare one rip-off to another, confirming only that other lemmings also paid too much for their houses. Their motive depends on who pays them. Appraisers who are paid by mortgage brokers and banks are motivated to give the appraisals that mortgage brokers and banks want to see. Appraisers that kill a deal by telling the truth do not get called back to do other appraisals.

Amazingly, all government house price statstics exclude houses with jumbo mortgages (mortgages too large for Fannie or Freddie to buy). This excludes about half of all houses in California from government statistics. So the government can report a price rise, but fail to mention that prices actually fell for the other 50% of houses in California that had jumbo loans.

Home Sweet Home

"It's not a house, it's a home."

FALSE. It's a house. Wherever one lives is home, be it a rental or not. Calling a house a "home" is a cynical manipulation of your emotions for profit. Don't let them do it. An agent once told me why agents invariably use the word "home" to refer to a house:

> A **house** is a wooden box that sits out in the rain and slowly rots. No one would buy if they really understood how much it's going to cost them in the long run. That's why we have to sell you a **home**, not a house.

Status

"If you don't own a house, you're a failure."

FALSE. Maximizing your assets and escaping the trap of mortgage debt is success. Most people have a hard time understanding this, but they do understand cash. You could show them your bank statements to prove you're way ahead of the game as a renter, but then they would probably just ask you for a loan!

The use of the status card is just one more well-known button that agents push to trick people into making foolish purchases. Don't let them do it.

> *Just as an unobserved tree falling in the forest makes no noise, a big beautiful home out in the lonely woods does little to increase status. The key to appreciating status is to have an audience – and there is no bigger audience than that of our major cities and the playgrounds of their wealthiest residents.*
> *– John Talbott, author of "Sell Now!"*

Affordability Is Good Now

"House ownership is near a record high, proving houses are affordable."

FALSE. The percentage of their house that most Americans actually own is near a record low, not a high. We do have a record number of people who have title to a house because they have dangerous levels of mortgage debt, but that is no cause to celebrate.

If you need a mortgage, you can't afford the house.

Owning Limits Your Monthly Payment

"Rents will rise, while a fixed house payment will not."

FALSE. Property taxes, maintenance, and insurance all go up every year, and interest rates on adjustable mortgages have nowhere to go but up.

When you pay a mortgage, your savings rate is reduced, making you more economically vulnerable. This seems OK as long as your equity is going up. Equity is theoretical money though, not cash in your pocket or bank account. The only way to get at that money without selling is to borrow against your house, increasing your debt.

Rents have not been rising in most places. In fact, they are being driven down by the glut of available housing because there has been way too much building going on due to artificially low interest rates.

When interest rates rise, then the value of your house falls, because fewer people can borrow enough to buy it. So even if your payment is fixed, your equity decreases.

Rents, however, are limited by the money people actually earn, not by how much they can borrow. Try walking into a bank and asking for a loan to pay your rent. You will be denied the loan. Since there are no loans to pay rent with, in order for rents to shoot up, salaries would have to shoot up first. But salaries are not likely to rise at all given the current unemployment rate.

People Buy On Emotion

"You failed to factor in emotion. More houses are sold on emotion than will ever be sold based on value. They buy all they can afford plus."

FALSE. Buyer emotion doesn't matter at all to the lenders, not on the way up or on the way down. Most people will borrow as much as they possibly can. The limiting factor is lending, not buyer emotion. There is no organization on earth that cares less about your emotions than your bank.

Baby Needs House

"Our new baby needs a house or it won't be happy."

FALSE. If you're pregnant and desperately want to buy a house for your new child, that's a perfectly normal feeling called "nesting." It is also a major cause of financial disaster! You certainly do not need a house for a baby. Babies don't need much space. A baby is utterly unaware of whether it lives in a rental or not.

Your baby will do better if you're not stressed out about a mortgage. You have five years before school quality becomes an issue, and at that point you can more easily move into the best school district as a renter than as an owner. Avoid debt and save your money so your child has a better start in life.

It's usually much cheaper to rent than to own the same size and quality house in neighborhoods with good school districts. In these neighborhoods, annual rents are often 3% of purchase price while mortgage rates are 5%, so **it costs nearly twice as much to borrow the money as it does to borrow the house**. Renters win and owners lose! Worse, total owner costs including taxes, maintenance, and insurance come to about 8% of purchase price, which is nearly three times the cost of renting and wipes out any tax benefit of owning.

I Just Want It

"I just want to own my own house."

TRUE. Most people do. There's nothing wrong with that. House ownership is great - unless you ruin your life paying for it. Buyers will get their chance when they have saved a fortune by renting and can pay cash when others cannot get a loan. Not only can cash buyers ask for a discount, but they also avoid all interest, points, and loan fees. This means they can own outright in less than half the time someone with a mortgage can pay it off.

But most people won't do the math, and they will try not to think about it during their grueling years of work trying to outrace their debt. They want to buy a house right now and to have someone tell them it is a smart decision. They don't want to hear about the true cost. But you're smarter than that.

Scams and Dirty Tricks

The real estate industry is rife with scams and dirty tricks, enough to fill an encyclopedia. Here are some of the most common ones.

Realtors® Claiming They Are "Free"

Nobody works for free, least of all Realtors®. This scam is written right into the questionable code of Realtor® "ethics":

> *Standard of Practice 12-1*
> *REALTORS® may use the term "free" and similar terms in their advertising and in other representations provided that all terms governing availability of the offered product or service are clearly disclosed at the same time.*

This means that Realtors® can "ethically" lie to buyers that 6% of the price of the house actually equals zero, as long as somewhere in the fine print they also disclose that they are being paid that 6% commission on the purchase price. And where does the purchase price money come from? From you of course! All commission money comes from buyers. No buyer, no money. When you buy, your broker gets paid from the money you spend. If you don't buy, your broker does not get paid.

Obviously, **you** are the one ultimately paying your agent, even if the agent is working for "free" and the commission check is written by the seller.

To make it even more painfully obvious, if you're so unwise as to "sign papers" with a buyer's agent, you'll probably find somewhere in the fine print that **you** are legally responsible for paying your "free" broker's commission if the seller does not pay.

The "free service" scam is central to trapping new buyers with mortgage debt. Since buyers hear the lie that Realtor® services are "free," they fail to look closely into the fine print or the inherent conflict of interest in the commission system.

Another way to look at Realtor® commissions is as a kickback scheme, where your own agent takes a bribe (his commission) for directing you to buy and perhaps overpay for a particular house. Kickbacks are normally illegal, but because the kickback arrangement is public and the NAR poisons our government with campaign donations, this particular form of kickback is kept legal, even though it obviously creates a direct conflict of interest between the buyer and his agent. The conflict is that your agent says that he represents your best interest, but his pay is maximized by betraying your best interest.

Either way you lose: If your agent gets paid by the seller, then he works for the seller, not for you. If your agent gets paid by you, then his services are not free.

Claiming That You Need An Agent

Not only do you not need an agent, your offers are **considerably weakened** when you have an agent, because the agent demands to get paid, taking money away from your offer. An offer without an agent is worth more than an offer with an agent.

Consider two offers on the same house, each for $200,000, but offer A includes the obligation to pay the buyer's agent, while offer B does not. Offer B wins, because it is worth more a little money to the seller, and a lot more money to the seller's agent, who can potentially get the entire 6% for himself.

Agents claim that you need them because they know how to complete all of the disclosure forms, but they don't mention that those forms are all publicly available. You can look them up and fill them all out yourself. It's not rocket surgery!

In an attempt to force you to pay Realtor® commissions, Realtors® may refuse to accept any offer unless it is on their copyrighted forms, and yet also refuse to give you permission to copy the forms unless you have a Realtor® agent. This is another reason why it is so important to **avoid all Realtors®** and go direct to the seller. The seller will undoubtedly be interested in at least hearing your offer, even if his agent is not.

Perversion of our laws has gotten to the point where it is illegal to pay someone in California even to fill out the forms for you unless they have a special license to fill out legal forms! Search for California law SB1418. This is of course presented as necessary to protect the public, while the actual intent is to prevent the public from escaping real estate commissions.

To ensure that your transaction is legal and safe, pay a lawyer for a few hours to look over your work. Unlike real estate agents, lawyers actually do have serious professional training, and unlike agents, lawyers have no financial interest in whether you buy a house or not. In Switzerland, buyers normally just hire a lawyer to complete any real estate transaction. They think it strange that anyone is naïve enough to believe that a "free" buyer's agent would honestly represent the buyer's best interest.

Agents use FUD (Fear, Uncertainty, and Doubt) to pry large amounts of money out of you. I'll admit it is one thing that they are very good at.

Showing You The Ugly Dogs First

Agents try to build your interest in quickly bidding on a mediocre house by making sure that the first few houses you see are truly crappy and overpriced.

The "anchoring" effect of seeing the ugly houses first is supposed to make you feel that the mediocre house that they show you next is not so bad. If you buy that one, the agent gets his commission out of you quickly, which was the goal all along.

Underpricing

Agents deliberately create false hope by "underpricing" houses, especially in California. Underpricing means advertising a price for a house well below what the seller would actually accept.

For example, say a seller's agent knows that house will probably go for $400,000. The agent places ads asking $300,000 instead, a price lower than the seller would actually accept. Such a classic bait-and-switch scam is illegal when selling toasters, or even cars, but not when selling houses, because of the huge donations that the NAR gives to legislators. California law entitles buyers to the lowest advertised price on any item, but again, an exception is made for real estate because of the corruption of our legislators by campaign donations.

Hopeful buyers are lured to look at the underpriced house thinking that they can afford it, and then are encouraged to spend hundreds or even thousands of dollars on inspections and title searches, only to find out later that the published asking price is not even close to a price that the buyer would accept. Buyers are then told to raise their bids to "protect their investment" in the property, meaning the money already sunk into the inspection and title search, perhaps thousands of dollars.

The goal is to first of all prevent buyers from knowing what a realistic price is, and secondly to get buyers to blindly bid against each other once they have already sunk money and emotion into getting that house.

There are four players in this game and three of them are against the buyer – the seller, the seller's agent and the buyer's agent. Yes, the buyer's own agent always works against the buyer, because there is no commission if there is no sale. There's a saying in Las Vegas:

> *There's a patsy in every game, and if you don't know who the patsy is, you're it.*

A suggestion from the Patrick.net forum for dealing with underpricing:

> *Just beat them at their own game: Beat out all other bidders by bidding unrealistically high, but be sure to have your offer contingent upon financing and house inspection. Since the bank won't finance you above the appraised value, you're then in a very*

strong position to re-negotiate the price far lower during escrow. The other bidders will be long gone.

Missing Price

Some real estate ads show the house, but don't list the price! Why would they do that? The seller's agent likes to have a missing price because it gives him complete power to do whatever is best for his own commission instead of what is best for the seller he supposedly represents.

It also allows the agent to size you up before stating a price, so that he can set the price to the maximum he thinks he can get out of you. It is especially important in such a situation to avoid stating the maximum you can afford. It's probably best not to even bother with any house that does not have a publicly listed asking price.

Missing Address

A house advertised without a specific address is another a way for agencies to size you up. Since you must call the agency to get the address, this means the agency has the opportunity to pump you for information like your maximum price, and to potentially get you to sign papers with their agency so that they can get both sides of the commission.

Renting Property Without Permission

If a bank asks an agent to sell a foreclosure property that is worth $200,000, but the agent lists it at $400,000, then the agent can be pretty sure no one will buy it. Since he has the key to the property, he can then rent it out secretly and pocket all the rent. The agent will keep collecting the illegal rent until the bank demands that the price be lowered, but by that time, the house may be damaged by the renters, or the price may have fallen. The bank may never even know the house was rented out.

An alternative scenario is when the seller's agent asks a price that's much too high just to keep the property on the market a long time, hoping that the seller gets discouraged and eventually dumps the house to himself or a friend for much less than its real value.

In either case, your own offer will simply be rejected or ignored because the agent has his own agenda.

Straw Buyers

Sometimes an owner colludes with an agent and a "straw buyer" to put his house on the market and then sell it to the straw buyer for much more than it's really worth. Once the bank issues the oversized loan to straw buyer, then the buyer, seller, and agent divvy up the loan money and disappear. The bank is stuck with a house worth much less than the amount of money it loaned.

Your own offer in such a case will again be rejected or ignored. You're just a prop in their play.

Faking Comps

The agent and the seller both have an incentive to fake recent comparable sales data to get the buyer to believe he must pay more. Do not attach any meaning to comps, even if you can confirm them with the county. As explained above, in some counties the recorded sale price is calculated from the transfer tax, say $1 per $1,000 of sale price. There is no rule against paying extra transfer tax. This means you have pay only $100 extra to cause your sale price to be publicly recorded as $100,000 higher than it actually was. This is very useful in pressuring the next buyer to pay more than necessary.

Of course you should never believe any comps from the MLS. There is no government agency checking that the MLS is correct.

Even accurately recorded sale prices can be a scam. There have been many cases where co-conspirators sold a house back and forth to each other repeatedly, at ever-escalating prices, to get "official" comps recorded at those prices. Why? Usually to pull the straw-buyer scam mentioned above.

A famous con man named John Drewe used to commission art forgeries and then infiltrate the archives and libraries of the art world, carefully unstitching the bindings of real art exhibition catalogs to insert false extra pages showing that his forged art had been displayed, say, 100 years ago in Vienna, and then stitching them up again. It never occurred to art buyers that anyone would go to such lengths, so the doctored exhibition catalogs were accepted as genuine for a long time. Remember this when someone shows you comps on a house you're interested in. The more money is involved, the more paranoid you need to be.

The only measure of house value that you can rely on is its rental value.

Faking The Dimensions

The actual dimensions of a house for sale may easily be misrepresented by the agent. You never know for sure unless you measure them yourself.

Faking The Sale

Sometimes you will be told verbally that your bid was accepted, but soon after that it is revealed that there was a higher bid, so you did not buy the house after all. This might be done because you were really being held in "reserve" as a backup buyer pending the other offer's finalization, or just to get you to think you have to raise your bid once again. Trying to get you to raise your bid this way is known as "gazumping" in England.

If your bid was not accepted in writing, it wasn't actually accepted at all.

Erasing Price History And Relisting

The MLS is a used-house sales tool designed to restrict access to critical market information in order to prevent the free market from working efficiently. There are actually many different MLS systems, usually one for each metro area, all unified by the desire to take as much money as possible from you.

All sorts of funny things happen in the MLS. For example, if a house just doesn't sell, the seller's agent can remove its history from the MLS so that you cannot see that it failed to sell. Then he relists the house at a lower price, so that you think it's on the market for the first time. Your agent can "prove" it's a new listing by showing the new MLS record to you: "See, here's the listing date, just came on the market. Better hurry and buy it, this one is hot."

The MLS resists including property for sale by owner, or through a discount broker, or bank-owned property, or extreme discounts from builders, or many other cases where you could save huge amounts of money. Those cheaper prices are often not in the system, because if you save money, agents lose money. Even if some cheaper properties are listed, your agent is not motivated to tell you about them if they require more work on his part, lower the probability of making a sale, or if they get him a smaller commission.

Faking Higher Offers

Your agent may actually draw up a fake competing bid and show it to you. He may even use real people's names on the fake bid, with or without their permission. Or he may just lie and verbally tell you there are other bids higher than your own.

Hiding Your Low Offer

If your agent thinks he can get more out of you to both raise his commission and give himself a better chance of making the sale, he can simply tell you that your offer was not accepted and that you need to raise your bid, without ever having shown your offer to the seller.

Taking Bribe To Hide Your Offer

Your agent may accept a bribe from another buyer to "lose" your offer, so that the seller never sees it. Or perhaps your agent "inadvertently" presents your offer at $100,000 below what you really bid. This has the same effect. Your agent gets the bribe, the other buyer gets a cheaper house, and you and the seller both lose.

Such bribery is not only possible under our current system, it's practically guaranteed when you blindly submit your offer only to your own agent and no one else. You have no proof that it was submitted to the seller. The fix for this problem is to mail your offer directly to the seller yourself, but that is probably prohibited by the papers you signed with your agent, and the seller may be prohibited from accepting directly-mailed offers by the papers that he signed with *his* agent.

Hiding Offer To Get Double Commission

Even without another buyer bribing your agent to hide your offer, the *seller's* agent may also happen to "lose" your offer if he has a lower offer from a buyer who is represented by his own agency. Double commission on a lower offer is still higher than a single commission on the higher offer.

Hiding Offer To Get Seller To Take Loss

The seller's agent may also "lose" your offer when he wants to pick up the property for himself or his friends for less than market value and then flip it. Banks are particularly vulnerable to this scam, since they have a hard time paying attention to the many foreclosures they are trying to sell.

If the seller's agent can convince the seller that there are no offers, then the agent himself or one of his friends can get a deal in buying it. This is one reason why it's hard to buy foreclosures directly from banks. The agents are trying to get a deal for themselves, so they tell the bank there are no offers at the current price.

Photoshop

Pictures in real estate ads are routinely photoshopped to remove power lines or bars on windows and to exaggerate space. An especially egregious form of exaggerating space is the use of unnaturally small furniture in a photo shoot to make a tiny room look bigger.

Advertising Agent Instead Of House

The real purpose of most real estate ads in the newspapers is to advertise the selling agent himself at the seller's expense, not to advertise the house. This is why the agent's face and name usually takes up much of the ad space.

Similarly, the real purpose of open houses is to collect the names and phone number of potential clients for the agent, whether buyers or sellers, not to advertise the house.

Kickbacks

Agents have the opportunity to get kickbacks from mortgage brokers, title companies, appraisers, inspectors, etc. in return for directing your business their way.

Mortgage brokers can also give away your maximum price or other critical information about you to your agent. This is not a problem if you simply don't have a mortgage broker or an agent.

Bribes

Remember that agents don't get paid unless you buy. This gives them a clear motive to pay a bribe to appraisers and inspectors so that they will not say anything that kills the deal like "The house is not worth nearly what you're offering" or "The house is badly infested with termites."

Instead of your agent's paying a bribe to an inspector to ignore problems, and then getting the money back as a kickback for referring your business, the two of them might just call it even at your expense: your agent sends you to the inspector, and the inspector agrees not to find anything bad about the house that might threaten the agent's commission. The only way to know for sure that your agent and an inspector are not in cahoots is to not have an commission-based agent at all.

A Trick Of Your Own

There is a way around the conflict of interest inherent in using a commission-based buyer's agent: let the seller's agent be your own agent too, just for that one house exclusively. Then the seller's agent has a big motive to lower the price just for you, because he will get double the commission if you buy it rather than some buyer with his own agent. Getting the both halves of the 6% commission on a lower price is still much more money than the agent's usual take of 3%.

This is called "dual agency" and would be considered deeply unethical in any other profession. Fortunately for you, the real estate industry is blind to ethical issues that reduce commissions. It's the same ethics-blindness that leads buyer's agents to assert that they get paid by the seller, but somehow still represent the buyer's best interest. You should use this blindness to your advantage if you can.

Having the seller's agent on your side also gives you inside information on how to best manipulate the seller into taking your lower offer. The seller's agent probably knows how motivated the seller is and what flaws there really are in the property. Using your own buyer's agent does not give you access to this critical information. But beware: the seller's agent might also tell the seller details about you.

What Should You Do?

How can you defend yourself from a corrupt system?

Be Paranoid

The more money is involved in any transaction, the more paranoid you should be about it. Buying a house is probably the biggest financial transaction of your life, so you should be very paranoid indeed. They are definitely out to get you.

To recognize the people who are out to get you, just follow the money. Don't take advice from agents, lenders, mortgage brokers, or anyone else who gets paid only if they convince you to buy. Do the math yourself and calculate what it would really cost you to own that house rather than to rent the equivalent.

Never Sign Any Agent Agreement

The first thing every agent will try to get you to do is to "sign papers" with them, meaning to sign a legal contract declaring them to be your agent, which entitles them to a commission if you buy property. Don't do it! Signing will only limit your options, weaken your offers, and set up the agent to take advantage of you.

Be aware that any papers you sign are likely to obligate you to pay the agent a commission if you buy *any* house for the term of the contract, even if the agent had nothing to do with it! Whether you buy an FSBO, or new construction, or even your own parents' house, you'll end up owing the agent a commission anyway.

Instead, just find a property or buyer on your own, have the property inspected, and get a real estate lawyer or perhaps an **hourly** agent to draw up or review your offer, which you then **personally** deliver to the seller. You can do it! It's not hard, and it's much safer for you. You are the one spending the money, so you are entitled to absolute control over the transaction.

Agents suck money out of the deal and monopolize and manipulate the critical information of exactly how many bids there are and at what prices. You cannot cancel your contract with an agent. Once you sign, you're screwed for the term of the contract, which could be several years.

An elderly Chinese lady in San Francisco by the name of Su Wan is reported to have cleverly played real estate agent greed to her advantage for many years now, by showing an agent her large bank account balance and telling him she might be interested in signing a contract with him. Once the agent is interested and thinks he is about to trap this little old lady, she asks to discuss the contract over an expensive dinner, at which she consistently "forgets" her wallet. The agent invariably picks up the tab, but Ms. Wan never signs any contract with any agent! She is also reported to have used this trick to get free rides around town, groceries, and designer clothing. Agents are so blinded by their own greed that they never see it coming.

Never Reveal Your Price Limit

Your agent will ask you the maximum you could possibly pay for a house. Since your agent is really working against your interests like everyone else above you in the food chain, giving away your maximum price is just asking for competing bids to magically rise to that price on every house you're interested in. **Never** let any agent or seller know your maximum price, or how much money you have in the bank, or any other significant financial detail about yourself. Just decide what a particular house is worth and stick to that number no matter what funny things happen with other bids.

If you must get a loan, do not get "pre-approved" for some amount and report that number to your agent! Pre-approval is another trick used by agents to find out how much money they might possibly extract from you by maximizing your debt. The term "pre-approval" doesn't even make sense. Either you're approved for a loan or you are not. It's fine to ask a bank how much you might comfortably borrow, but don't tell anyone that number. It's your secret.

Hire Your Own Independent Inspector

Never hire any inspector referred by someone with an interest in your buying the house. Always hire your own inspector.

See http://patrick.net/home_inspectors.php for a list of inspectors near you.

Do not buy anything that wasn't built properly, no matter how cheap it gets. Many foreclosures are houses that weren't built properly, and these houses tend to be foreclosed over and over again. Lots of houses are ugly, but an ugly but well built house is often the best deal.

Favor FSBOs

Every FSBO (For Sale By Owner) house is a more straightforward deal than any house for sale by an agent, just because you can go directly to the owner and negotiate on your own. You also get to skip paying the commission. Maybe the owner will be reasonable in his asking price and maybe not, but at least the layer of harmful obscurity created by real estate agents is removed.

Sellers should **always** sell their house FSBO and **never** sign a contract with any agent. Not only do FSBO sellers get the safety of real visibility and control over one of the biggest transactions of their lives, they also come out financially **ahead** of sellers who use an agent, because they get the same or better average selling price and also save the 6% commission that the agents would otherwise demand. Search for the 2007 study by Northwestern University on FSBO transactions.

Realtors® hate FSBOs because FSBOs prove that agent services are unnecessary. In 2004. a Realtor® working as Commissioner of the California Department of Real Estate (notice any conflict of interest there?) unethically attempted to block even the *display* of FSBO listings on the web without a real estate license. See the case FSBO vs Zinneman. This was obviously a misuse of state government office in an attempt to force the public to pay Realtor® commissions. Fortunately, the case was dismissed as a violation of the First Amendment, but it shows that Realtors® have infiltrated our government and will attempt to use public office against the public interest.

Do Not Rush

Your agent will frequently tell you that you must rush and put your "best and highest offer" on the table right now, before some other buyer snatches the house, perhaps even before you've had it inspected! He may also arrange for the owner's phone to ring off the hook with bogus offers just so that you will "accidentally" overhear them while you're viewing the house. Don't fall for it.

Time is on your side. Baby boomers are retiring. There are 70 million Americans born between 1945-1960. One-third have zero retirement savings. The only money they have is equity in a house, so they must sell. This will add yet another flood of houses to the market, driving prices down even more.

If you want to buy, why hurry? Save your cash and don't jump into anything. All your savings on the price of a house are tax-free earnings! For Californians: buy **after** the next huge earthquake, **not** before.

Signing a 30-year commitment is crazy. No one can guarantee that their income will continue uninterrupted for 30 years. Maybe 30-year mortgages worked when jobs were for life, but those days are long gone.

There is a huge glut of empty new houses. Builders are being forced to drop prices even faster than owners, because builders must sell to keep their business going. They need the money now. Builders have huge excess inventory, and more houses are completed each day, favoring those who wait.

Do Not Overpay

It is safe to buy only when the price is low enough

so that you could rent out the house and make a profit. *Buy a house only when a landlord would buy it.* Then you'll know it's pretty safe to buy for yourself because then rent could cover the mortgage and ownership expenses if necessary, eliminating most of your risk.

The landlord rule of thumb is to divide annual rent by the purchase price for the house. This gives you a gross percentage return on your investment.

If the gross annual rent is 3% of the purchase price, then **do not buy**; the price is too high.

If the gross annual rent is 6% of the purchase price, then it's a borderline case.

If the gross annual rent is 9% of the purchase price, then it's OK to buy; the price is reasonable compared to rent.

So for example, it's borderline to pay $200,000 for a house that would cost you $1,000 per month to rent. That's $12,000 per year in rent. If you buy it with a 6% annual ownership costs, that's $12,000 per year as well, so it works out about the same.

It is foolish to pay $400,000 for that same house, because renting it would cost only half as much per year, and renters are completely safe from falling housing prices.

Although there is no way to be sure that rents won't fall, the local employment rate is a good hint of the direction rents are likely to go. If unemployment is rising, rents are probably going to fall, and vice versa.

It's a terrible time to buy when interest rates are low. House prices rose as interest rates fell, and house prices will fall as interest rates rise without a strong increase in jobs, because a fixed monthly payment covers a smaller mortgage at a higher interest rate. Since interest rates have nowhere to go but up, prices have nowhere to go but down.

It is far better to pay a low price with a high interest rate than a high price with a low interest rate, even if the monthly payment is the same either way.

- A low price lets you pay it all off instead of being a debt-slave for the rest of your life.
- As interest rates fall, real estate prices generally rise.
- Your property taxes will be lower with a low purchase price.
- Paying a high price now may trap you "under water", meaning you'll have a mortgage debt larger than the value of the house. Then you will not be able to refinance because you'll have no equity, and will not be able to sell without a loss. Even if you get a long-term fixed rate mortgage, when rates inevitably go

up your equity will go down. Paying a low price minimizes your damage.

- You can refinance when you buy at a higher interest rate and rates fall, but current buyers will never be able to refinance for a lower interest rate in the future. Rates are already as low as they can go.

Deliver Offer To Seller Personally

If you make an offer, **deliver the offer to the seller yourself** so that your agent or the seller's agent can't hide it. Do not give it to the seller's agent.

Be sure to include broad contingencies written into your offer, so that you can back out of buying easily if trouble arises. This could be as simple as saying that you reserve the right to withdraw your offer within 30 days if you disapprove of the inspection results. There will always be some reason you can disapprove of the inspection results.

Pay Cash

Mortgage interest generally **doubles** the actual cost of the house to you. It takes an unlikely amount of appreciation to keep up with that size of a drain on your cash.

When you pay cash, you're completely free from bank control over your life, you avoid interest, origination fees, and points, and you save many hours of paperwork time. You're also more likely to get a low offer accepted when you pay cash.

The way to win the game is to have cash on hand when others cannot get a loan. You do not want to be bidding your hard-earned savings against fools who are bankrupting themselves with debt.

Long Term Lease

A long-term rental with a multiple-year lease is a good way to get stability with the economic benefits of renting. Many landlords are quite willing to negotiate a long term lease, or at least the option to renew your lease for a very modest rent increase. Make sure they can't raise the rent much during the lease term, and make sure there is only a small penalty for ending the lease early. Even if you sign a normal 1-year lease, landlords hate finding new tenants, so they are not inclined to raise the rent much on existing good tenants. This means you can probably stay a long time without much of a rent increase.

Walk Away

If you already own and can't sell without a loss, it may be best to just walk away and free yourself from mortgage slavery. It's perfectly legal and moral according to the terms of the mortgage, but there are a couple of catches.

First, if someone loans you money and you don't pay it back, the IRS normally considers that money to be part of your income. Fortunately, the IRS has temporarily stopped taxing forgiven debt, so you may be able to walk away without owing anything! From the IRS website:

> *If you owe a debt to someone else and they cancel or forgive that debt, the canceled amount may be taxable.*
>
> *The Mortgage Debt Relief Act of 2007 generally allows taxpayers to exclude income from the discharge of debt on their principal residence. Debt reduced through mortgage restructuring, as well as mortgage debt forgiven in connection with a foreclosure, qualifies for the relief.*
>
> *This provision applies to debt forgiven in calendar years 2007 through 2012. Up to $2 million of forgiven debt is eligible for this exclusion ($1 million if married filing separately). The exclusion does not apply if the discharge is due to services performed for the lender or any other reason not directly related to a decline in the home's value or the taxpayer's financial condition.*

Second, your bank may be able to come after you for the money you didn't pay back. It depends on whether your loan was "recourse" or "non-recourse." In the non-recourse case, the deal is simply that you can stop paying the mortgage and give back the house at any time.

California is a non-recourse state, which means that if you stop paying your original mortgage and walk away, they can't take any of your other assets. In some other states all loans are recourse and the bank can always come after your personal assets. Talk to a lawyer before walking away. *If you refinanced, you may have given up your non-recourse status*

During the big housing crash, many people in California housing developments would buy a nearby second house of the same model as their first house, but for half their current loan amount. Then they would move and default on their first loan. If their first loan had non-recourse status, they got to live in the same model house in the same neighborhood for half of their previous debt.

If You're A Realtor®

If you're a Realtor®, you should quit being one immediately. Do not pay the NAR dues, just quit. It may be difficult and painful to admit that you belonged to such an organization, but there is still time to repair your self-esteem. Spread the word about the political manipulations of the NAR and the fallacy of "free" advice from a commission-based salesman. Find an honest and helpful way to make a living, perhaps as an hourly agent. It may not be easy, but you'll be happy to sleep with a clean conscience every night.

Calculating Fair Price

Annual income twenty pounds, annual expenditure nineteen six, result happiness. Annual income twenty pounds, annual expenditure twenty pound ought and six, result misery.
–Charles Dickens in David Copperfield

A house has a fair price. Agents will tell you that "whatever someone will pay" is the fair price, but that's very wrong. Just because someone else will overpay for a house does not mean that you should too.

The fair price really depends on what your alternatives are. It depends on how much it costs you to do one thing versus another.

To live somewhere, you have to pay something. There's no way around that unless someone else is paying for you.

The value of a house depends entirely on what it would rent for. It does not depend on what you paid for it, or on how much you spent to build it. If you can save money every month by renting the same quality house in a nearby location, then it is foolish to buy at that asking price. The price is just too high.

Rents, in turn, depend on salaries. At some point during the housing bubble, the cost of owning shot right past the cost of renting. Owners were losing money, month after month, for years, on a real cash flow basis relative to renting. But they didn't care because they thought their equity was increasing. They could even refinance at the greater valuation implied by "comps" – sale prices of similar properties nearby – and pull money out to cover their monthly shortfall.

That worked until it didn't, and America woke up with a dreadful hangover, still ongoing. What's worse is that many powerful financial interests are determined to make sure that we never sober up.

Two Kinds Of Rent

Everyone always pays rent, whether they own or not. Your two rental options are to pay *rent for a house* or to pay interest, which is just *rent on money*. Even if you don't borrow any money to buy, you're still paying rent because you're losing the interest (rent on your money) that you could have had if you had invested your money elsewhere. So the question is how to minimize your rent.

If you borrow the entire purchase price to buy a house, that's pure interest to the bank -- renting money from the bank.

You could put some money down, but that's just a

combination of the two kinds of rent: losing rent on your money and paying rent on the bank's money.

Say you can pay cash for a $250,000 house that would rent for $1,000 per month. Should you buy it? That depends on current interest rates.

$250,000 invested at the current interest rate will produce a certain amount of income for you each year. Ignoring taxes for now, say you can get 5% by investing your cash. This means that $250,000 will return $12,500 per year, since $250,000 x 5% = $12,500.

So if you have $250,000 and need a place to live, your choice is between these two options for the coming year:

- Buy the house for $250,000 and don't pay any rent.
- Invest the $250,000 at 5%, and pay $1,000 rent per month to live in a house.

Which one is better? In the first case, you're not getting any investment income, but not paying any rent either. Owning outright means giving up interest rather than paying interest, a different kind of loss, but a loss nonetheless. In the second case, you're getting $12,500 in interest income from your bonds, but paying out $12,000 in rent. $12,500 income - $12,000 rent = $500

So you would be $500 better off in the coming

year as a renter.

Borrowing Does Not Help

"But I don't have $250,000 to pay for a house. I would have to borrow it."

In that case, it's an even worse deal to buy a house. Let's start with the simplest case: an interest-only mortgage. To borrow $250,000, let's say you have to pay 6% when points and fees are included.

The interest on $250,000 at 6% is $15,000 per year. In effect, that's the yearly rent you have to pay to use the money. These are now your two options for the coming year:

- Buy the house for $250,000 in borrowed money, and pay $15,000 in interest.
- Pay $1,000 rent per month to live in a house, so $12,000 per year.

Buying would cost $15,000 in interest, but you could pay only $12,000 in rent. So you would be $3,000 better off per year as a renter.

Downpayment Doesn't Help Much

"What if I put down 20%? Would that help?"

Not much. That's just a combination of the two cases above, both of which show it is worse to buy than to rent. So it would still be worse to buy.

If you have 20% of $250,000, that's $50,000. If

you could get 5% by putting that $50,000 in bonds rather than in a house, that would be $2,500 per year in interest income.

These are now your two options for the coming year:

- Buy the house for $200,000 in borrowed money plus your $50,000 downpayment, and pay 6% interest on the $200,000, which is $12,000.
- Pay $12,000 rent per year to live in a house, but collect $2,500 in bond interest.

So buying would cost you $12,000 per year, and renting would also cost $12,000 per year, but if you rent, you get the $2,500 in interest on your $50,000. So you would be $2,500 better off as a renter.

Conventional Mortgage

"But I'll get a conventional 30-year mortgage, not an interest-only mortgage."

That's still just a combination of the first two cases. As you pay off the debt, the interest you pay each month decreases, but the principal you are putting into your house may still be a poor investment relative to your other options, the stock market, or bonds.

Deduction Doesn't Help Most People

"What about the tax deduction?"

There is no tax deduction. There is only an *income* deduction. You may deduct mortgage interest from your gross taxable income but not from your taxes.

In any case, there is no benefit unless you pay more mortgage interest than your standard deduction of $11,900. Every married couple gets a $11,900 standard deduction, just for breathing. You reduced your income by the amount of interest. You can pay interest with pre-tax money, but you really spent it and it's really gone.

At the upper end of the market there are limits imposed by the AMT and the $1 million limit on mortgage debt. If you make enough money, the AMT is going to limit how much you can deduct in total. The $1 million limit on mortgage debt means that the maximum you can deduct is, say, $60,000 in interest at 6%. No matter how much you make you can't deduct more than that much interest from your income.

While it's true that you can reduce your taxable income by the amount of mortgage interest you pay, up to those limits, the other costs of owning eliminate that advantage. Not to mention the fact that other bidders get the same deduction, so they bid up the price to negate the advantage for everyone. Only the banks win, because they increase their interest payments from everyone.

Take the previous case, but say that you pay that $12,000 in interest with pre-tax money, meaning your interest was fully deductible. You've really paid that money, and it's really gone, but since you didn't have to pay income tax on that money before spending it on interest, it's not quite as painful. At a 28% marginal income tax rate, it's only 72% as painful as paying $12,000 in post tax money. So let's say your interest payment is only $8,640, which is 72% of $12,000.

But we should also consider that you'll have to pay property tax, maintenance, and insurance on your house, forever. Property tax is typically 1.5%, maintenance is about 1.5%, and let's say you can get house insurance for $1,000 per year. So for your $250,000 house, that's $3,750 property tax, $3,750 maintenance, and $1,000 insurance, a total of $8,500.

These are now your two options for the coming year:

- Buy the house for $200,000 in borrowed money plus your $50,000 downpayment, and pay $8,640 interest after income deduction, plus $8,500 in property tax, maintenance, and insurance, a total of $17,140.
- Pay $12,000 rent per year to live in a house, but collect $2,500 in bond interest. Property tax, maintenance, and insurance are paid by your landlord, so you have a net

cost of $9,500 as a renter.

Buying would cost you $17,140 per year, but renting would cost you $9,500. So you would be $7,640 better off as a renter. That's not even considering the standard income deduction, which allows a renting couple to deduct $11,900 anyway.

Appreciation Is Uncertain

"But haven't houses always appreciated in the long term?"

Appreciation is house price inflation. House price inflation tracks general inflation in the long term. Prices did rise a lot from 2001 to 2005, but that was very unusual, caused by exceptionally low interest rates and very lax lending standards. Prices peaked in 2005, and have been falling since then. If prices fall another 5% in the coming year, as they did last year, then your choice is this one:

- A cost of $17,140 from the previous case, plus a 5% loss on your $250,000 house. That 5% loss is $12,500, for a total owner's cost of $29,640.
- The renter has the same $9,500 cost as before, and does not care about the depreciation of the building he's in.

So you would be $20,140 better off as a renter.

If you look at the very long term, houses have been the **worst** investment available to the general public. Whether you look at 10, 20, or 30 years, stocks have always been the best investment, returning about 7% beyond inflation annually, followed by bonds at about 3%, with housing always dead last at about 1.3%.

Taxability Of Gains

"But the bond interest is taxable, so you don't really get 3%."

Buying a bond is just the simplest possible investment example and not necessarily the best one. You can actually get 3% and defer taxes for decades, or not even have to pay tax at all. There are a few well-known ways:

- Buy your bonds in your 401K account. 401K's are tax-deferred until retirement.
- Buy your bonds in your Roth IRA. The principal you put into your Roth IRA is post-tax, but all the accumulated earnings are completely tax free, as long as you keep them in the account until retirement.
- Buy US Treasuries in a taxable account. Though the rates are a bit lower than CD's, there is no state tax on US Treasury bond interest.
- Buy municipal bonds from your state. The interest rate is even lower, but there is no state or federal tax on the interest.
- Buy and hold solid dividend-paying stocks.

If you hold a stock for more than a year, the tax rate on any gains is only 15%. And you can put off any capital gains tax indefinitely just by continuing to hold the stock.

- Buy and hold index funds. Index funds, which are mutual funds that mirror stock market indexes like the Dow or S&P 500, have historically risen much faster than housing. And you can hold them indefinitely and put off the capital gains tax as long as you like.

- Pay off debt. If you pay off credit card debt and avoid 20% interest rates, you're way ahead of even the best professional investors. If a penny saved is a penny earned, then 20% saved is 20% earned. Actually, it's even better than that because it's tax free.

- Pay rent in advance for a discount. If you can get a 5% discount by paying an extra month's rent in advance, you've earned 5% in one month. That's an annualized rate of 60%, which is an insanely great return.

What About Leverage?

"My agent told me how leverage is the secret to building wealth in real estate."

When you hear someone telling you why you

should maximize your leverage in real estate, run, do not walk, *run* to the nearest exit!

Leverage means using debt to amplify gain. Most people forget that **debt amplifies losses** as well.

Leverage is a bet that the appreciation will be greater than the cost of borrowing. For example, if you buy a $100,000 house borrowing at 6% with nothing down, and the house goes up 5% in a year, are you $5,000 ahead? Maybe. You spent $6,000 in interest, plus all the others costs of owning, but you got the use of the house plus the $5,000. For many years this bet worked, so people assumed it would continue that way forever.

The problem is that **leverage works both ways**. What if the house goes down 5%? Then you've spent your $6,000 in interest, *and* you've lost $5,000.

Leverage is the evil that bankrupts the most people during every housing market downturn.

Warren Buffet says the greatest threats to personal wealth are "liquor and leverage."

What About Inflation?

"Real estate is protected from inflation."

Ignoring bubbles and crashes, most of the long-term gain in housing prices has actually been inflation. What you really care about is after-inflation returns. A glance at the after-inflation returns of various investments shows that housing has the lowest real return of any kind of investment, while suffering from very high risk.

Banks take inflation into account when lending you the money to buy a house. You can be sure you will be compensating the bank for the expected rate of inflation. On the other hand, it's possible that the banks will be wrong and salary inflation will skyrocket, greatly reducing the value of the debt that borrowers owe, meaning that borrowers don't have to spend as many years as obedient servants working for the bank. In that case, owners do win, and banks lose. This happened in the S&L crisis of the 1980's, but then the banks' losses were just forced onto taxpayers as usual.

Rules Of Thumb

"How does this compare to valuation rules of thumb?"

At banks, the rule of thumb is that a safe mortgage Is a *maximum* of 3 times the buyer's annual income with a 20% downpayment.

The landlords' rule of thumb is that a safe price is set by the rental market; annual gross rent should be at least 9% of the purchase price, or else the price is just too high. Landlords never borrow at a rate higher than the gross rent divided by the property cost. If the gross rent is only 3% per year, they would never borrow at 5% because they'd be certain of losing at least 2% per year, and much more with expenses.

In affluent areas, *both* those safety rules are still being routinely violated. Buyers are still borrowing 7 times their income with tiny downpayments, and gross rents are still only 3% of purchase price, even after recent price declines. Renting is a cash business that proves what people can really pay based on their salary, not how much they can borrow. Salaries and rents prove that affluent neighborhoods are still in a huge housing bubble. Anyone who bought a comparable "bargain" in those areas recently is already sitting on a very painful loss because they went by comps and not by rental values.

The higher-end housing market is now set up for a huge crash in prices, since there is no more fake paper equity from the sale of a previously overvalued property and because the market for securitized jumbo loans is dead. Without that fake equity, most people don't have the money needed for a down payment on an expensive house. It takes a very long time indeed to save up for a 20% downpayment when you're still making mortgage payments on an underwater house.

On the other hand, in some poor neighborhoods, prices are now so low that gross rents exceed 10% of price. Housing is a bargain for buyers there.

Prices there could still fall yet more if unemployment rises or interest rates go up, but neighborhoods where the cost of owning is below the cost of renting have no bubble anymore.

Anything else?

Well, yes, there is also the 6% that the agents will take in commissions. That reduces the resale value of a $250K house to you by another $15,000. There are also thousands of dollars in closing fees, and PMI (Private Mortgage Insurance) if you can't come up with the 20% downpayment.

Long-Term Solutions

Call Housing Inflation What It Is

The press should stop characterizing higher house prices as better. Higher house prices are not an "improvement" and lower prices are not a "worsening" of the housing market. Higher house prices are simply inflation, and inflation is bad for buyers.

When the price of a product like a gallon of gas or a loaf of bread goes up, the purchasing power of hard-earned money is destroyed, and the government comes under pressure to stop the inflation. Rising rents are also counted as inflation, yet *house price* inflation is never counted in any government inflation metrics, nor is there ever any pressure on the government to stop it. Why is that?

The reason is that housing inflation seems to magically increase the wealth of current owners, so those owners like that particular inflation a lot. Obviously no new wealth is being produced from house price increases, so where where does the owner's gain come from?

The owner's gain comes from an unearned **transfer of wealth** from young families just starting out. Those young families have to burden themselves with unsustainable mortgage debt to come up with the cash to give sellers. This is a tragedy and government should have no part in encouraging it. The government should classify housing inflation as what it really is, the most harmful form of inflation that we have, and all government policy should be oriented toward achieving lower house prices and less mortgage debt.

Most Americans directly benefit by a decrease in house prices. Only the banks and elderly sellers who are downsizing benefit from increased mortgage debt. Elderly sellers depend on young families' getting themselves into debt. Less debt for the young means lower selling prices for the old.

Even current owners benefit from a decrease in house prices. If they ever want to upgrade, higher prices mean they'll just have to pay more for the next house, while lower prices mean they will get a discount when they buy. A 10% fall in their current small house and a 10% fall in the bigger more expensive house they want to buy means they will come out ahead. Owners who want to upgrade should be firmly on the side of lower prices.

Help Correct Reporters

Help correct reporters when they use obviously biased terminology. When reporters say that housing prices "improved" when they went up, tell them paying more for a house is no improvement to you and ask them to issue a correction to their article. Get your friends to do this too. Please also correct any reporter or agent who says that a high bidder "won" a house as if it were something good to pay more for a house than anyone else would.

Ask reporters to stop being cheerleaders for mortgage debt.

No Public Guarantees For Private Debt

We should abolish all government guarantees on mortgage debt.

People in the Midwest and South (where the average house price is less than $175,000) should not be forced via their tax dollars to guarantee $729,750 jumbo Fannie and Freddie mortgages for Californians. They cannot get that guarantee for their own mortgages. The injustice is galling.

It is very profitable to get people into debt. Those profits result in political pressure to pass laws encouraging mortgage debt. For everyone above the buyer on the food chain – from seller to real estate agent to bank to Congress, the White House, and the Federal Reserve – there is a strong interest in getting young and inexperience families deeply into debt. Once in debt, new buyers, too, become part of the problem – they need to find new housing victims if they want to eventually sell at a profit.

Thus we have the mortgage interest deduction, Fannie Mae, Freddie Mac, the Federal Housing Administration (FHA), and other harmful government programs, all of which serve primarily to increase the amount of mortgage debt, which increases prices, negating the increased buying power of that debt. Since most people don't do math very well and will take on as much mortgage debt as they can, this government facilitation simply results in higher house prices.

Higher prices negate any benefit to the buyer – but they do benefit people higher up the food chain. Those profits at the expense of the buyer get funneled into campaign contributions that keep the housing trap in place, or make it even more pernicious.

No Mortgage Interest Deduction

We should completely eliminate the mortgage-interest deduction, which costs the government $400 billion per year in tax revenue. **The mortgage interest deduction directly harms all buyers** by keeping prices higher than they would otherwise be, costing buyers just as much in extra purchase cost as they save on taxes.

The creation of the mortgage interest deduction caused debt and prices to rise to a higher level as everyone used the subsidy to borrow more for a house. It was politically easy to do, since it benefited banks and current owners, but it's politically hard to undo, since it will harm banks and current owners to take prices back down to their unsubsidized free market level.

Subsidies harm consumers by increasing prices. Subsidies benefit the first few recipients, but the sellers quickly catch on to the new source of revenue and increase prices to negate that benefit for all subsequent recipients. All subsidies flow directly to businesses as excess profit at public expense. This is true especially for housing and health care subsidies, and the businesses that benefit from these subsidies spend lavishly on lobbying and campaign contributions to make sure the subsidies continue, in the name of the "public good" even though subsidies are obviously a public harm

The public believes that the income deduction benefits them. They are very wrong about that, but what the public believes, no matter how wrong, is reality to politicians. No politician wants to be accused of "taking away" a public benefit.

Buyers should be rioting in the streets, demanding an end to all mortgage subsidies. Canada and Australia have no mortgage-interest deduction for owner-occupied housing. It can be done.

Encouraging debt has resulted in disaster. Instead, we should promote savings, and outright

106

ownership without any debt at all, in every generation.

How can we make lower house prices our official government policy? How can we completely eliminate the mortgage interest deduction which drives up housing costs and discriminates against renters? How can we wipe out Fannie Mae, Freddie Mac, the FHA, and other agencies whose job it is to enslave Americans to mortgage debt?

As Patrick.net reader Sean Olender put it:

> *Many people have forgotten that the number one restriction on their future freedom to do what they want, when they want, and to go where they want isn't the Iraqis, or Iranians, or North Koreans – it's **their mortgage lender.***

Public Bids On Housing

The real estate system in America is all about deception, about preventing the buyer from getting complete and accurate information. There is no free market in housing because bids on houses are **never** published.

Public bidding is necessary for a free market in housing. We do not have a free market in housing right now. Not only are bids are secret, but bidder names are hidden so that bidders can't speak with each other. Fake bids deceive buyers into overpaying, and real bids are hidden from sellers when they do not benefit the seller's agent. The secrecy and lies in housing bids make it impossible to know the true market. All bids on a house should be public information, along with the address being bid on, the date and time, the amount, the bidder name, and the name of the bank which validated the bid. Bidders should have to prove real financial means to that bank in the amount of the bid. Fake bids should be a serious crime.

Legally Binding Offers To Sell

If you see a toaster advertised for $40 and you go to the store and are told you must pay $60 instead, the seller is committing a crime called "bait and switch". But this dishonesty is standard business practice in real estate, especially on the coasts. Houses are advertised for a price less than what the seller would accept to deceive buyers about the true state of the market and to encourage blind bidding over the asking price. As with anything else for sale, an advertised asking price should be a *legally binding offer to sell at that price*. If there is no higher bid in 30 days, the seller should be obligated to sell to any bidder at that asking price. The seller should not be able to raise the price before the 30 days are up.

Eliminate Comps As Meaningless

Lending regulations should eliminate comparable sales ("comps") as meaningless. All lending should be based by law on the true value of a house, namely, what it would cost to rent the equivalent house. If lending were never beyond the true rental value of a house, there were be very few foreclosures, if any, since the owner could always rent out the house to cover the mortgage.

No Empty Houses

Foreclosures don't ruin neighborhoods – empty houses do.

Banks should be heavily fined for leaving foreclosed property empty and deteriorating. If the banks won't take care of their houses quickly, the title should be auctioned off to people who will occupy and take care of them. Yes, even if the auction lowers comps or forces the bank to take a loss.

If an empty house is in limbo, with no payments being made and yet not foreclosed on because the bank doesn't want to take maintenance costs, the delinquent owner and the bank should both quickly be stripped of all ownership claims and the house should be auctioned off.

Houses remain empty only because prices are too high and because banks don't want to admit a loss on their balance sheets. If prices were allowed to fall enough so that salaries can easily cover the cost of owning, people would move in and take care of the houses. In areas without jobs, the first priority should be jobs.

To prevent a justified foreclosure is also to prevent a deserving family from buying that house at a low price.

Publicly Financed Elections

> *The first truth is that the liberty of a democracy is not safe if the people tolerate the growth of private power to a point where it becomes stronger than their democratic state itself. That, in its essence, is fascism – ownership of government by an individual, by a group, or by any other controlling private power.*
> *– Franklin D. Roosevelt*

What we have now in this country is a system of legalized bribery. Wealthy special interests like the NAR and their lobbyists in RPAC donate to congressional campaigns with full expectation of a large return on their bribe. Namely, they expect that the congressmen who take their money will vote the "right" way on laws. Legislators at both the state and federal level will let lobbyists **write** the laws, and then sign those laws without even bothering to read them!

Unfortunately, a congressman really don't have much of a choice because of our campaign finance system. If the other candidate is getting big bribes from the NAR, he is himself forced to do whatever it takes to get that money too, or he will be at a disadvantage in the election. Money buys elections in America. This is explained very clearly in a video called "The Best Government Money Can Buy":

http://www.thebestgovernmentmoneycanbuy.com/

The solution is **public** campaign finance, a ban on private campaign contributions, and an end to the rotating door between lobbying firms and congressional staff. Taxpayers would pay for campaigns, but then even the little guy would have a chance to get elected if his ideas were good.

Of course everyone in Congress got elected under the current system, so they are not inclined to change it unless the public demands change.

End Proposition 13 In California

Proposition 13 limits property tax increases to only a tiny amount per year, unless the house changes hands, at which point the property tax resets to a percentage of the sales price. Prop 13 was presented as a way to protect poor old people from property tax increases, but the **real** goal was to shift property taxes away from the wealthy and onto everyone else, especially onto new buyers. This is why Prop 13 was designed with no means test and why it also applies to businesses. Businesses never get old, so they can effectively pay less and less property tax forever as the Fed inflates away the currency while the dollar amount on their tax bill remains nearly constant.

Two identical houses right next to each other in California often have dramatically different tax rates due to Prop 13, with wealthy long-time owners paying nearly nothing, while struggling young families are forced to pay higher property taxes to cover the shortfall left by their rich tax-evading neighbors. It's long past time to repeal Prop 13.

The Georgist Land Value Tax

> *They hang the man and flog the woman who steals the goose from off the common, but let the greater criminal loose who steals the common from under the goose.*

We could eliminate all income tax, sales tax, and all other taxes with a single 6% annual tax on land values instead. No one created the land, and no one can hide it. Unlike the income tax and sales tax, the land value tax does not penalize work or commerce. It gives you the easy ability to control your own tax rate by using less land. It is extremely simple and fair. It is the best possible tax.

The land value tax would also keep house prices under control and would discourage speculation in land. We would all be much better off – except large wealthy landowners who extract unearned land rents from the rest of us.

These are the ideas of Henry George. Look up Henry George in the Wikipedia for more information.

Spread The Word

If you agree with at least some of the ideas in this book, please loan it to friends, because people need to know the arguments against mortgage debt and the ever-hungry predators in the food chain will never tell them.

If you have to bid against ignorant buyers who do not see how they are being set up for The Housing Trap, then both you and the other buyer lose. It is much better to explain the situation to other buyers, hopefully with a copy of this book! A good understanding can reduce house prices for both of you.

Visit the Patrick.net forum for an active community of folks who refuse to step into the housing trap. They are entertaining and often have good answer for your questions.

Please ask your local library to order this book. It also makes an excellent gift!

About Patrick Killelea and Patrick.net

Patrick is a programmer living in Menlo Park, California. Patrick started the http://patrick.net website in 2004 with the mission of making the housing market fair for the buyer. The public has taken note and currently daily readership exceeds 18,000 for his website and e-mail newsletter. Patrick has been interviewed on Nightline, NPR, and in the Wall Street Journal.